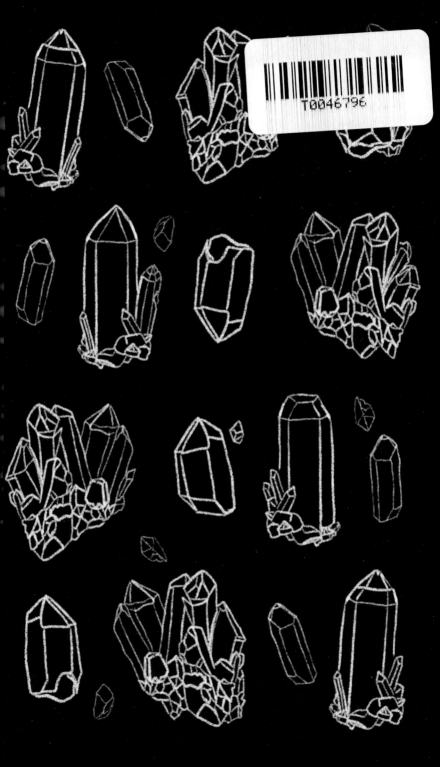

# PERSEPHONE MADE ME DO IT

poems, prose, art

## TRISTA MATEER

central
avenue
PUBLISHING

2023

Published by Central Avenue Publishing, an imprint of Central Avenue Marketing Ltd.
www.centralavenuepublishing.com

**PERSEPHONE MADE ME DO IT**

978-1-77168-291-6 (pbk)
978-1-77168-292-3 (ebk)

Published in Canada

Printed in United States of America

1. POETRY / Women Authors    2. POETRY / Subject & Themes - General


10 9 8 7 6 5 4 3 2 1

Keep up with Central Avenue

*for who we were*
*and who we had to become*

# CONTENTS

# PERSEPHONE

Greek goddess of death, destruction, spring, nature, and agriculture; Queen of the Underworld.

*sacred to her (non-exhaustive list)*
pomegranates, honey, grain, bats, smoky quartz, obsidian, citrine, peridot, bees, wildflowers

# NAMES TO KNOW

The Underworld: Dark realm of the Greek afterlife that houses the souls of the dead; includes the Fields of Mourning, the Elysian Fields, Asphodel Meadows, Tartarus, River Styx, River Lethe, etc.

| | |
|---|---|
| Cerberus: | Three-headed watchdog of the Underworld |
| Demeter: | Goddess of the harvest, fertility, and the cycle of life and death; mother of Persephone |
| Hades: | Lord of the Underworld, brother of Zeus, husband of Persephone, god of wealth and death |
| Hecate: | Goddess of witchcraft, necromancy, ghosts |
| Hermes: | Messenger, soul guide, god of speed, etc. |
| Zeus: | King of the Olympians, father of Persephone |
| Charon: | The ferryman of the Underworld, son of Nyx |
| Eve: | The first woman, according to Abrahamic religions |
| Helios: | Personification and god of the sun |
| Heracles: | A Greek hero, son of Zeus |
| Nyx: | Personification and goddess of night |

destruction

chaos

awakening

The Tower

# INTRODUCTION

My mother kisses
my cheek and says
I look just like her.

Then she stands
in front of the mirror
and destroys herself.

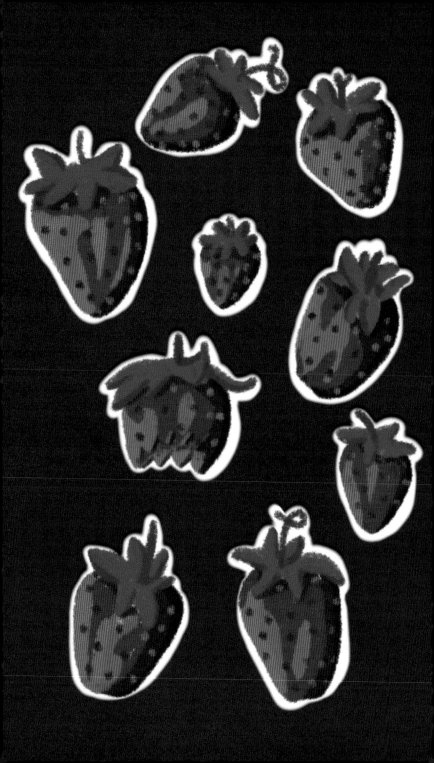

## THE FEAR

i am too much.
i am too much.

i am too much in all the ways
a person can be too much.
too big.
too loud.
too curious.
too angry.
wanting too much.
needing too much.
always being left.
not good enough to keep.
too much to love.
too much to handle.
i am too much.
i am too much.
and somehow

i will still
never be enough.

As a child,
I chased intangible things:
wishes and fairies and stardust.

When I grew up,
I fabricated love out of
phone calls and distance.

I've never wanted what
I could actually touch.

*LOVE FEELS*
*OTHERWORLDLY NOW*
*AFTER HOLDING IT AT*
*SUCH A DISTANCE*

Year after year
we grow further apart.
You embrace me
like you're hugging
a stranger.
You miss the girl
I used to be
but you refuse to admit
she is gone.

I feel like I just spent six months underground.

# THE URGE

to dream of pomegranate and honey, to kiss the mirror with lipstick on, to stop and smell the roses, to take a punch, to knock some teeth out, to sneak into your mother's room and try on her perfume, to run away from home, to be reborn, to be abandoned, to steal into God's garden and strip the trees bare, to thirst for knowledge, to look for more, to want and want and want and want, to become something else, to cocoon, to transform, to miss a home you can never return to, to return anyway, to shower with the lights off, to be indelicate and deliberate, to kick, to scream, to bleed, to be, to hold hands with yourself, to outgrow every box they put you in, to get knocked down and then get up again and again and again and again and again and

# THE DREAM GOES LIKE THIS

Everything is too much. Everything is too real. And it's reaching for me and it wants me and my heart is beating out of my chest—and then I am awake. The nightmare is over. The fear is fading. I open my eyes and see my bedroom. I try to breathe a sigh of relief, but the relief never comes. I can't move. There's a weight on my chest and it's pinning me down. It's pinning me down. Down. Down. I can't handle that anymore. Being stuck somewhere. Being restrained. I am screaming inside my head. I squeeze my eyes shut so hard I see stars, but I know I have to open them again eventually—and when I do, the mirror in the corner of the room is glowing.

I take a few deep breaths and look again only to see the same thing. There's golden light spilling out from my bedroom mirror. Eventually the weight lifts from my chest and my breathing evens out and I know that I could roll over and go back to sleep, but how can I not get up and look? How can I not touch it?

When I reach the mirror, I don't see my face at all. I see spring. Sun and clouds and wildflowers close enough to smell. I glance back at the rest of my room but everything looks the same. Curiosity gets the best of me. It always does. I reach out to pluck the nearest wildflower from the mirror but as soon as I touch it, my entire world falls away and I am standing alone in a meadow.

A meadow full of other mirrors. Some of them show my face and some of them don't. A number of mirrors are smashed and jagged. A few are boarded up. Most show other places. A silver standing mirror houses a forest. A pink vanity mirror has a bit of high tide pouring out. I think I've been here before.

"Wasn't sure I'd see you again, girl," a voice calls to me. I don't recognize the woman speaking, but she feels familiar.

"Do I know you?" I ask, stepping closer. Her mirror is white and ornate but the inside is a swirl of darkness. I hear a river rushing behind her. There's a torch in her hand, but most of her is obscured.

I reach out to run my fingers along the frame of her mirror. It's made of carved bone.

new path

surrender

fresh perspectives

THE HANGED MAN

# PERSEPHONE AIRS HER GRIEVANCES

They called me *girl*.

And they called me Kore,
which was just another way
of saying girl.

And they mixed me up
with my sisters
after they gave me sisters.

And when they called me
the name of my mother,
I still answered.

I always answer.

Sometimes you get used to answering
no matter what they call you.

Unlike other god-children
I was not granted real status or power
at birth.

I didn't get to crawl into the lap of Zeus
and tell him who I wanted to be.

I wasn't allowed
to live on the Mountain.
I wasn't even allowed
to call myself an Olympian.

They sent me to the fields where Mother lived. I grew up with the flowers and the weeds. I grew up in the dirt. A wild little thing, running on honey and cake and mother's love.

Father's absence was rarely spoken of,
but it was felt.

Of course I wanted what I couldn't have.
Everyone does.

When I was old enough, I began helping my mother with her duties. The wheat and the grain and the corn. The sowing and the growing and the harvesting. The feeding of the earth.

We were worshipped in different ways across the land. Festivals. Dancing. Feasting. Sacrifice too. Ritual baths and sacred rites. We promised a better afterlife to the locals, and they praised us above all others.

As we controlled what lived,
we controlled what died.

## THEY SAY

The Lord of the Underworld
went to Zeus first,

and it was my father
who suggested me as a bride
for his brother.

It was my father
who suggested my abduction.

Mother wasn't told.

I wasn't told.

## THIS MUCH IS TRUE

I was sickly sweet and young,
high on the joy of living,
flower-picking in the meadow.


He waited until I was alone.

He stole up behind me.

He pinned me to the earth.

And then he dragged me beneath it.

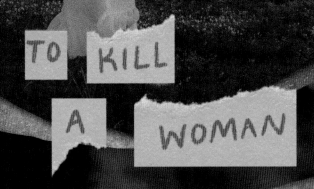

THERE ARE MANY DIFFERENT WAYS

TO KILL A WOMAN

Men have been abducting women
since the dawn of time,
so maybe

I shouldn't have been surprised
when it happened to me.

And still,
with my face smashed down in the dirt,
I was surprised.

I thought I would be safe,
being God's Daughter.
I thought I would be the exception
instead of the rule.

ALL GIRLS
MUST LEAVE
THE SAFETY
OF MOTHER'S
MEADOW
EVENTUALLY


BUT


NOT LIKE THAT

No matter what they say,

I made the best out of a bad situation.
That's what survivors do.

Sweet Maiden.

Unnamed One.

Chaos Bringer.

Destroyer.

THE END OF EVERY SURVIVAL STORY:

I wasn't ready to become what I had to become.

I don't know what you've heard.

I'm not that girl anymore.

She died.

She is Death.

Dread
Persephone

feared by mortals

and gods

# I KNOW YOU, girL.

# I HaVe beeN WaTCHiNG you FoR YouR eNTiRe LiFe.

# THE POET AIRS HER GRIEVANCES

In the dream

my childhood home burns

to the ground.

It is a good dream.

Some daughters
must survive their fathers
the way hikers survive
encounters with bears.

Stay still long enough
and maybe he won't see you.

Pray he is not hungry.

# JUST LIKE YOUR MOTHER

If you had a father like mine,
there was a day when he stopped
looking at you like you were a child
and started
looking at you like you were a woman.

I was a princess
until I was old enough to be a bitch.

I USED TO THINK IT WAS
HIS ANGER THAT LIVED
INSIDE OF ME

BUT NOW I KNOW

IT'S MINE

I bargained away
my pink and lace
at eleven,

rolled my eyes
at glitter
even when no one else
was looking.

For years
I spit in the face
of
everything pretty.

I spit in my own face.

I wanted to be
one of The Untouchables.

I wanted to be
King of the Mountain.

## SLUMP

& I never made my homes out of places. Not
physical places, anyway. I made my homes
out of paper places. Nothing ever felt safer
or more real than the worlds inside my
head. I grew up on books. Hungry and
never satiated. I grew up ravenous
for words, which of course is why
I started writing them down. Tried
making homes out of people for a
while but it didn't work out. Now
I make poems out of them instead
and still don't have anyplace
I feel like I belong. These
days it's hard to even find
the peace of mind to pick
up a book and slip into it.
I feel like I've been stuck
on the other side for so
long I don't remember
how to get back over
there. Through the
words. Into the
story. Into that
other place
where it's
safe.

I don't need you to tell me
that I am loved or whole or good.

I need you to watch me
wade into the river of my misery
and sit down at the bottom.

I need you to watch me
hold my breath.

19

Flowers and rain.
Fire and blood.
I feel nothing
and everything
all at once.

Sometimes I go out looking
for the girl I used to be,
but I can never find her.

The face in the mirror
isn't wrong. It's just
not what I remember.

at least we have the memories

## CRUMBS

Can't I just get a little bit of love?
Can't I try a bite?
Can't I at least have a taste?

## THE MARRIAGE TALK

At dinner my mother says, *It's not about being submissive;*
*it's about being smart. Learn what's worth fighting about.*
*The braver you are, the more you're going to get hurt.*

> I wonder if all women must try not to be hurt
> by the men they love. And how is it love if it's so
> tinged with fear?

The moon fills and empties.
The seasons cycle too,
fast as teens on the bike path.
I am becoming my mother.
I catch it in the mirror.
Dim the lights.

I see the world for what it is,
and it exhausts me.

I DON'T NEED ANYTHING

I DON'T NEED ANYONE

create the life you want

Queen of Pentacles

# PERSEPHONE LAMENTS

## STUBBORN GIRL,

You need everyone.
You need everything.

You're just afraid
you won't get it all
in the end.

At some point
all girls feel like they are too much.

Too soft.
Too loud.
Too needy.
Too angry.
Too human.

*YOU ARE A POETIC MESS*
*OF CONTRADICTIONS.*

*WHY WOULD YOU EVER*
*WANT TO BE ANYTHING LESS?*

# IT'S BEEN SAID THAT I WANTED TO LEAVE

Of course I wanted to leave.
I wanted things my mother didn't understand.
I wanted things I didn't understand.
I wanted freedom
and I wanted power.

I STILL WASN'T "ASKING FOR IT"
CURSE EVERY CARELESS PEN THAT SAYS OTHERWISE

IT'S NOT YOUR FAULT
IT'S NOT YOUR FAULT
IT'S NOT YOUR FAULT
IT'S NOT YOUR FAULT
IT'S NOT YOUR FAULT
IT'S NOT YOUR FAULT

I long for
the simplicity
of my girlhood.

I wasn't some sleeping princess
waiting to be kissed awake.
I wasn't a dull blade in need of sharpening.
I wasn't the embodiment of innocence.
I wasn't passive.
I wasn't just sitting in the meadow,
letting life happen to me
until the day
he arrived in his chariot
to whisk me away.

I had a life
before he stole it from me.
I was someone different,
but I was still someone
who mattered.

*GRIEF FOR THE GIRL*
*I USED TO BE.*

*WE'LL NEVER KNOW*
*WHAT SHE COULD HAVE*
*BECOME.*

My mother
would have
destroyed
the earth
to save me.

She tried to.

sometimes grief makes more sense
than reason / they say Demeter let
everything die when she discovered
me missing / she stopped eating and
drinking / she stood on the Mountain
and screamed at Zeus until her throat
was raw / the ground cracked and the
crops died and the people died too /

until everyone was forced to mourn

as she mourned

Mother missed me so much
she invented winter.

ALL DAUGHTERS WANT THEIR
MOTHERS TO SAVE THEM

ALL MOTHERS KNOW THEY
CANNOT SAVE THEIR DAUGHTERS

ALL MOTHERS WANT THEIR
DAUGHTERS TO SAVE THEM

ALL DAUGHTERS KNOW THEY
CANNOT SAVE THEIR MOTHERS

## THE WAY THEY TELL IT,

The Lord of the Underworld
trapped me in Tartarus
long enough
to trick me into eating
a handful of pomegranate seeds,

tying me eternally
to his realm
for a few months every year,

      but everyone knows
      you can't eat in the Underworld
      and still expect to leave.

      They teach it to children.

# HELL-BENT

There was no leaving for me.
Not really.

I knew it the moment
we went under-world.
I was buried.

Mother's tears
wouldn't bring me back whole.
They couldn't.

Many mothers have tried.

Kore was dead.
Persephone's what was left.

# THE POMEGRANATE AND THE PACT

I saw an opportunity
and I took it
and I swallowed it

and I savored the taste.

# POEM FOR DEMETER, AFTER THE FACT

Mama, what did you expect me to do?
He offered me his kingdom.
An Olympian title.
A place in the pantheon.
Power beyond imagination.

He offered me a chance
to be remembered
by my name.

we
always
find
our
way
back
to
each
other

you're disconnected

be still

listen to your inner voice

the high priestess

# THE POET LAMENTS

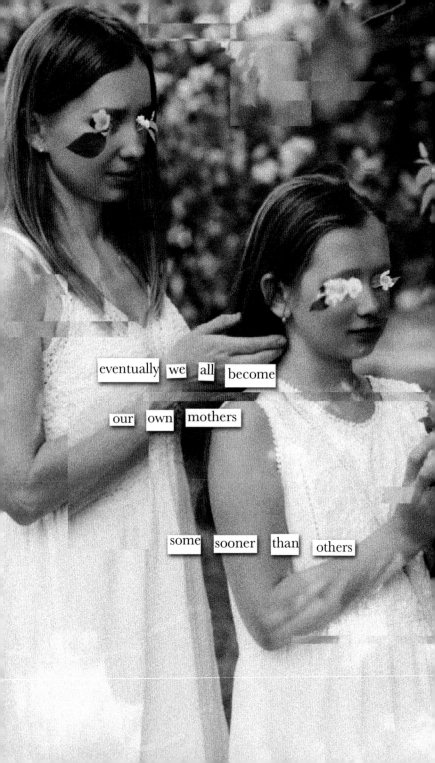

eventually we all become

our own mothers

some sooner than others

# POEM IN WHICH I BEG ON MY KNEES

"So I'll get to return to her one day? We'll understand each other? We'll fix it? Or make it better? Or make it bearable?"

Persephone doesn't answer.

"I'll return to my mother the same way you return to yours every year. And everything will be just as it was when I was a girl. Right?"

Persephone doesn't answer.

a girl needs a mother

      a girl needs something to run from
      and something to run toward

a mortal enemy and a god that looks like her

She says,
*How can you*
*be mad at me?*
*I created you.*

I say,
*That is why*
*I am angry.*

# HOME FOR THE HOLIDAYS

I am no longer myself around her. I am something else. Something smaller and afraid. When I see her, the grown woman in me shatters and out stumbles this inept little thing with no boundaries and aching hands. I need to be held. All of a sudden I need to be held. All of a sudden I am remembering that I need to be held. I am young again and wanting something my mother cannot give me.

MOM I WISH
YOU FIXED THIS
INSTEAD OF
GIVING IT TO ME

## WHEN MY FATHER ISN'T AROUND, MY MOTHER BECOMES A PERSON AGAIN

Relaxes her shoulders. Breathes. Eats a piece of bread. Laughs. Tells me about her life. Pours a glass of wine. Cries. Laughs again. Tells me every horrible thing that's ever happened to her. Asks what I want for dinner.

People ask me
where I'm from
and I don't know
what to say.
Can you be
from a place
if it
spits you out?
If it forces you

to go?
Can you belong
to an unsafe place?
I had a hometown
once,
and then I didn't
anymore.
Something broke
in the middle
of that story,
and it was me.

# GIVE ME BACK MY HOMETOWN

I grew up in a small town, listening to country songs about other small towns. My radio played a constant stream of women singing about one-way tickets and wide-open spaces. Needing to get some new guitar strings and a spot on the next Greyhound bus. Needing to get away. Needing to outrun. And I thought: Why? I love this place. All the yellow oxeye daisies by the train tracks. Main Street. All those long conversations in vacant parking lots. The coffee shop with Open Mic nights where I fell in love more than once. Cornfields and the bar I grew up in. But small towns can turn so quickly into cages.

Trauma paints fresh red x's over all the common ground. The grocery store. The coffee shop. The bar. The man and his hands everywhere. I served the mother of my rapist at the restaurant where I worked. More than once. Before I quit my job. Served him too. Had to walk up and introduce myself. Had to say my name like he didn't remember it. I had to ask him what he wanted and then I had to give it to him.

Again.

Big trauma in a small town turns everything against you. Eventually there are more reasons to run than to stay. You might return for the holidays, but it never feels like coming home.

And it never will again.

so, okay

here's where I'm stuck:

how do I forgive *myself*
for wanting you
and for believing you were good
and for waiting for you
for so fucking long?

I find myself
envious of boyhood.

What's it like
charging through life,
breaking things

instead of being
what gets broken?

"You don't want to end up like your mother, do you?"

"No, I would rather die and yes of course I do."

I HATE BEING SEEN

I NEED TO BE SEEN

I DON'T FEEL LIKE I EXIST WHEN I'M NOT BEING LOOKED AT

IF A GIRL DIES WHEN NO ONE IS LOOKING AT HER WHAT WAS IT ALL FOR

IF A TREE FALLS IN A FOREST AND NO ONE IS AROUND TO SEE THE BREAKDOWN DID IT EVEN HAPPEN DID IT EVEN MATTER

ISN'T LIFE A PERFORMANCE

DOESN'T EVERYONE FEEL THAT WAY

AND IF NOT
WHAT THEN

My world ended and I did not die.
Perhaps I should have.
It would have been easier.

Loneliness has always been kinder to me
than men have been.

# FORGIVE AND FORGET

If you don't let me be angry now,
I'm never going to get rid of it.
It will burn me up and hollow me out
so it can live inside me forever.

I hate that every man I know
has done something horrible
to a woman / and I hate
that she has forgiven him.

Mother,
make me good again.
Make me okay. Help me
up and fix my hair. Cup my
face and paint the world gold
again. I can't do it on my own.
I'm ready to admit it. Can you
hear me? Can't you hear me?
I'm ready to come home now.
I'm ready to go back to
what I was before.

AND
YOU
POUND
YOUR FISTS

AND
YOU
WEEP ON
THE FLOOR

BUT
THERE
IS

NO
GOING
BACK

• keep trying • keep going • strength • courage

Nine of Wands

# PERSEPHONE SPEAKS ON RESILIENCE

In little ways,
girls are always
dying        and
coming alive again.

people called her wrathful
people called her destructive

but my mother was right to be angry

Zeus knew where I was.
Helios saw all that happened under the sun.
Hermes and Hecate and Charon and Nyx
all moved freely between the Upper World
and the Under.

They knew where I was.

No one bothered to intervene until they were
inconvenienced by my mother's grief.

They say Hermes led me out of the dark.
They say Hecate led me out of the dark.
They say I led myself out of the dark
and everything was good again
and I embraced my mother
and the earth rejoiced

but that doesn't make sense, does it?
You don't get to go through Hell
and come out the same.

I can return to the meadow,
but I can never be that girl again.
Not knowing what I know now.

I deserved better.

I deserved more.

# I CAN'T
# HAVE
# JUSTICE

# SO I
# SETTLE

# FOR
# POWER

Now I split my time
between the realm of the living
and the realm of the dead.

My mother is always waiting
for me to return to her,
and I am always waiting
for me to return to myself.

# MOTHER ASKS WHAT I'VE DONE WITH MY LIFE AND I SAY,

Comforted the souls of the lost.

Gossiped with the dead.

Turned a few girls into comets. They needed space.

Helped some heroes find their way.

Pitied a poet but still made a bet he couldn't win.

Fought with my sister over a boy.

Lent my dog to Heracles.

Made a man out of clay. Just one of those days.

Invented mint. Don't ask me how.

Tormented the men who came looking for me.

Started a plague or two. I don't keep track.

## CERBERUS

Oh, you can change him!
Bring him inside and teach him
not to bite

but you must live with the fact
that he has probably
bitten others.

if I am selfish for wanting

to keep one foot in heaven

and one foot in hell

then I am selfish

so what talk shit

I still get what I want

*YOU CANNOT*
*PLEASE*
*EVERYONE.*

*YOU WERE NOT*
*MADE TO PLEASE*
*ANYONE.*

The unkillable woman.
Watch how she crawls
back from every grave
ever dug for her.
Watch how she endures
and endures and endures.
Watch how she overcomes.

*I AM NO LONGER*
*ASKING FOR PERMISSION*
*OR FORGIVENESS.*

## THE GIRL YOU USED TO BE

Whenever you can,
you must force yourself
to look back at her.
Reassure her
that you are still there.
Treat her with kindness.
Do not let her
become a memory.
Let her live through you.
Let her live.

I may never be that girl again but she is still alive as long as I remember her

*SOMETIMES WOMEN MUST*
*SWALLOW DARKNESS*
*IN ORDER TO GROW,*
*TO CHANGE,*
*TO DEFEND THEMSELVES.*

*I AM THE DARKNESS.*

What do you really know
about the women
who came before you?
Not your mother.
Not your grandmother.
Before that.
The nameless ones.
The women only remembered
by birth dates
and number of sons.
The women who suffered
so that you could live.

hope

purpose

renewal

# THE STAR

THE POET IS IRREPRESSIBLE

*I MIGHT SCREAM*

*AND CRY*

*AND CURSE TOO MUCH*

*AND STAY UP TOO LATE*

*AND KISS THE WRONG PEOPLE*

*AND RUIN MYSELF*

*AND DROWN IN MY OWN SADNESS*

*AND CRACK THE EARTH RIGHT IN HALF*


*BUT I WILL NEVER*
*BE RELEGATED TO A BLANK PAGE*
*LIKE THE WOMEN BEFORE ME*


*YOU WILL KNOW MY FUCKING NAME*

I am angrier than I've ever been
but

    I am also full of love.

It's been so long,
every bad thing that happened to me
feels like it happened to some other girl.
And yet
the body remembers.
You can see it when I flinch.

You hold the key to your own cage.
You are forbidden from using it,
but you don't remember who told you that
or why you're still listening.

*FINE,*
*I WILL UNHINGE MY JAW*
*AND TAKE A BITE OF THE WORLD*
*LIKE IT'S A RIPE PEACH*
*AND I WON'T EVEN*
*WIPE THE JUICE FROM MY FACE*

*FINE,*
*I WILL LIVE*

*I REFUSE TO*
*MAKE MYSELF*
*PALATABLE.*

*I WILL NOT*
*GO DOWN*
*EASY.*

## SHE'S . . . DIFFICULT TO WORK WITH

Difficult women know they deserve better.
Difficult women stand up for themselves.
Difficult women call you on your bullshit.
Difficult women take up space.
Difficult women raise their voices.
Difficult women are not afraid of leaving.
Or of you.

Eventually

I always find

my way back

to myself

In the name of Persephone,
I embrace my duality.
The day and night in me
no longer frighten me.

Sometimes I'm angry at my mother
when I should be angry at God.
She is closer and more real.

I swear
I didn't mean to
write so many poems
about my mother,

but how could I stop?
And how can you blame me?

I open my mouth and
her voice drips out.

What happened to spring?
*Winter came.*

What happened to you?
*Winter came.*

God put the fruit on the tree.
Made the tree.
Made the fruit.
God put Eve in front of the tree.
Made Eve.
Made the devil.
Made the knowledge.
Made the garden.
God made the cage
before he trapped her inside of it.
Punished her for finding the key.
Always planned on her finding the key.
There was no other way forward.

Now God wants to talk to me about forgiveness,
but God is the one who needs to be forgiven.

IF I'M HONEST ABOUT HOW I'M FEELING...
IT MIGHT MAKE
PEOPLE
UNCOMFORTABLE
BUT IT MIGHT
ALSO
KEEP ME ALIVE

When I say I'm angry,
they keep trying to talk me into
forgiveness.

The truth is, I did forgive him.
The first time.
Not the second.

The truth is, my friend forgave him
before that
and so did his ex
and so did that girl
from seventh-grade science.

What has forgiveness done
except elongate the line
of broken women
in his path?

who would I have been
if I'd never said yes to that date

if trauma hadn't tried to eat me alive

if I hadn't known grief

if I hadn't
known
you?

grief for the girl I used to be

& grief for the years I missed her
but couldn't name the feeling

& grief for the remembering

I am waiting for
the damage to heal—
hoping I will
crawl out of the
trauma as
a new person.

So this is it? This is my story now?
The Dying Girl.
The Dead Girl.
The Bitch.
The Survivor.

Don't I ever get to be anything else?

Don't I ever get to be myself again?

explore
express
embrace

curiosity
possibility

Page of CUPS

# PERSEPHONE: RECLAIMING

You're going to miss her forever.

I will not allow my life
to be defined
by what happened to me
in that meadow.

Let my name appear on the page
without his.

Even if it's just once.

Even if it's just here.

Let me spin my own tale.
Allow me that courtesy.
Rewrite it tolerable.
Make peace by making art.

arranged marriage without my consent
rape and kidnapping
stockholm and roses
forbidden love and elopement

my husband, the villain
    no, my father
    no, my mother

*ALL DETAILS CHANGE*
*OVER TIME.*

*ARGUING THE TRUTH*
*IS SENSELESS.*

*TELL THE STORY*
*YOU CAN LIVE WITH.*

She who locks eyes
with the devil
and swallows him whole.

She who walks into Hell
and makes it her kingdom
instead of her torment.

Let me tell you a story.
Girl lost in the labyrinth.
Girl stolen by demons.
Girl dragged down to Hell.

Let me tell you a story.
Girl was made to be wanted.
Girl was made to be lonely.
Girl invents sin.

Let me tell you a story.
Girl befriends darkness.
Girl eludes definition.
Girl creates life.

Let me tell you a story.
Girl tends to God's garden.
Girl eats God's fruit.
Girl becomes King.

# MAIDEN? MOTHER? CRONE?

Aphrodite

Ariadne

Artemis

Brigid

Demeter

Enodia

Ereshkigal

Eve

Gaia

Hagne

Hecate

Inanna

Isis

Kali

Kore

Mary

Melinoë

Nephthys

Nestis

Nyx

Pandora

Proserpina

Rhea

Shakti

Sita

Sophia

Venus

You

WE ARE ALL THE SAME WOMAN.

WE ARE ALWAYS THE SAME WOMAN.

WE ARE ALWAYS THE SAME WOMAN

TELLING THE SAME STORY.

TELLING PIECES OF THE SAME STORY.

TELLING STORIES SO SIMILAR

THEY MAY AS WELL BE THE SAME.

LET ME CALL YOU BY MY NAME.

The old stories don't even
call me by a name,
and you think that's where
I come from?

You think a man
wrote me into being
with his pen?

YOU THINK HE HANDED ME A CROWN? I WAS QUEEN OF DEATH BEFORE THE GREEK PANTHEON EVEN EXISTED.

I've been chewed up and spat out and repackaged so many times you don't even realize how often you've heard my story.

I've been a thousand women.

I've lived a thousand lives.

The Greek poets rewrote me innocent and beautiful, cast me in the role of daughter, and made me passive. An object, lusted after until I was taken. Seduced by a serpent. Assaulted by my uncle first and my father second. Tied to both of them for eternity. But they handed me God's fruit and called it freedom and named me Queen. I took what was offered and ran with it.

The church rewrote me stubborn and naked, stripped of all my hard edges. Said there was no way I could have existed before Man. Gave me one of his ribs as proof. They sent me to the garden and made me Motherless. Seduced by the same snake. They offered me God's fruit just like before, but this time they punished me for taking it.

And then they used my story
as an excuse to punish *every woman forever.*

## WOMAN

They know what you used to be
what you could be
what you should be

and they hate you for it.

I am ancient

like death is ancient.

They wanted to shackle my power.
Make you forget.
Make you believe I am not dangerous.

They wanted to pull back the curtain
and let you see the girl I was,
in hopes that you would no longer fear me.

They painted
a portrait of me
lounging
in a field of wildflowers.
Put it on display.
Acted like
that's all I was.

Sweet.
And pink.
And naïve.
And bleeding.

*GIRL, YOU CAN TRY*
*TO MAKE YOURSELF*
*SMALL ENOUGH*
*TO COMFORT*
*A MAN'S EGO*

*BUT YOU WILL*
*NEVER*
*BE*

*SMALL ENOUGH*

Couldn't conceive
of a woman with power
so they rewrote me without it,
stripped me of my titles
and made me walk through fire
to reclaim them,
wrote me wounded
and then twisted the knife.
Which version came first?
Which version matters?
You want to know
what happened to me?
I was a girl.
Now I am a god.

Every woman
goes through Hell
and comes out again
changed.

Let your contradictions
and complexity

stand in defiance

of a world that trained you
to be bite-sized
and easily consumable.

*YOU'VE WASTED YEARS*
*GROWING APART FROM YOURSELF.*

*LET GO OF THE PERFORMANCE*
*OF WOMANHOOD.*

*STOP PRETENDING TO BE*
*WHAT YOU'RE NOT.*

With one hand
you must hold on to the girl
you used to be,

and with the other hand
you must embrace
whatever
you are becoming.

## PARADOX

Life is terrible and beautiful
and shorter than you wish
and longer than you know.
You have plenty of time.
Don't waste a minute.

# THE DREAM ENDS LIKE THIS

Persephone is staring at herself in the mirror. Persephone is staring at her younger self in the mirror. A girl in a meadow. Like a ghost or a dream. Close enough to touch. Persephone drops her torches and reaches her hand through the mirror, feels the familiar breeze of the Elysian Fields, smells the flowers of the dead. She takes the girl's hand.

"You still have so much life in front of you," Persephone says. She feels a tinge of jealousy but she doesn't speak it. "You're going to be amazing."

"It's time for me to leave now, isn't it?" the girl asks. Persephone nods solemnly. The girl sulks. She turns her back to the mirror, eyes searching for the path home.

"One thing before you go," Persephone says. She steps out into the sun, onto the field, wild hair and black robes billowing behind her. She pulls the girl tightly to her chest.

*I love you.*
*And I miss you.*
*And I will be missing you forever, girl.*

# ACKNOWLEDGMENTS

I have to thank my readers first. This series wouldn't exist without you. Thank you for being here. And thank you so much to everyone who is still picking up copies of *Aphrodite Made Me Do It* and suggesting it to their friends. I wouldn't be able to do what I do without you! Thank you to Michelle Halket and the teams over at Central Avenue & IPG for giving this book a home.

Thanks to Lauren Zaknoun for her wonderful cover work, Jessica Peirce for her indispensable edits (as always), and the lovely Nikita Gill as well for her constant support.

And thank you to everyone I forced to read early drafts of this book before I could bear to send it in for editing. I appreciate you immensely.

# CREDITS

creative direction: Trista Mateer

editing: Jessica Peirce

proofreading: Molly Winter

photography: pexels

cover design: Lauren Zaknoun

interior illustrations: Trista Mateer

interior design: Michelle Halket

publisher: Central Avenue Publishing

sales & distribution: IPG

foreign & audio rights: Linda Migalti,
Susan Schulman Literary Agency

Trista Mateer is the bestselling author of multiple poetry collections including *Aphrodite Made Me Do It,* *I Swear Somewhere This Works*, and sapphic cult-favorite *Honeybee*. She writes about love and everything else.

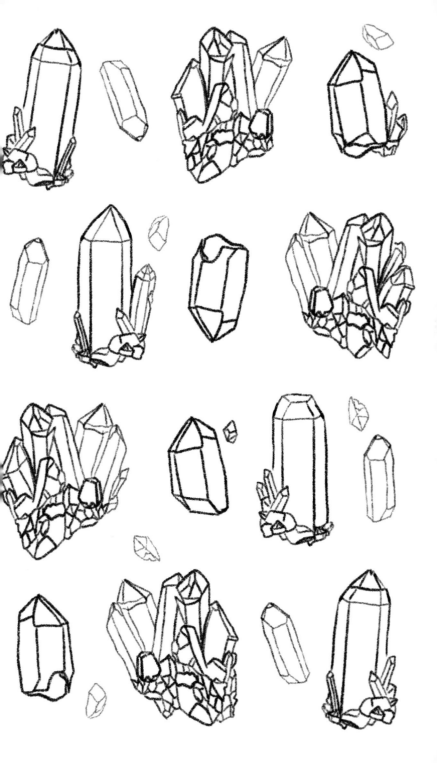